SHE LEFT LIKE SUNDAY

VIV

A Book By:
FOREVER SHININGS
Instagram - @forevershinings.co
forevershinings1@gmail.com

Book Title: She Left Like Sunday

Book Author: Viv

Published By: FOREVER SHININGS

First Edition: 2025

ISBN: 978-93-5605-461-5

She left without saying goodbye.

So I wrote a book she'll never forget.

VIV

This book contains tears you never saw,

goodbyes that weren't said,

and truths no one let me speak.

If you're still healing, read it slowly.

If you're still waiting for them to come back — maybe skip the last page.

VIV

DEDICATION

To my parents and my dear siblings----
for loving me quietly while I loved one who didn't.
For still seeing me when I was lost.

To my mates-
who stayed back while I was lost in a love that did not return.
I'm sorry I made you see me sink.
and thank you
for holding on to the me
I kept trying to save.

VIV

NOTE TO READERS

This book is not for those who moved on very easily
It's for those who stayed too long,
who forgave too much,
who said sorry for their feelings
and then wept in silence when love did not come.

If you've begged one to stay—
but said it in poems for your voice was too low,
this book is for you.

If you've been told you were "too much,"
when you were just loving one
who gave you scraps—
this book is for you.

I didn't write this for your cure.
I wrote it so you'd know you're not alone
in still checking if their name shows
on a phone that's quiet for ages.

Welcome to the pages where I broke.

Take your time.

It's fine to cry here.

This is a safe spot

for those who never found closure.

PROLOGUE

I did not pen this book as I wished to.
I penned it as I had to.

For when you yell your heart out and no one hears—
you start to write to show you were here.

This is not poetry.
This is how love looks when it fades slow,
no noise,
no cause,
no one to note.

It began with small bits—
long replies, short hugs, soft talks.
I kept forgiving this,
hoped that if I stayed soft,
you'd recall why I was key.

But soft boys fall first in love tales.
and I think this was mine.

VIV

I’ve written many poems,
but none could bring you back.
I've said “I’m sorry” more than my own name,
and still,
you gave my heart to one
I once warned you of.

So if you hold this book,
you're not reading to know me—
you’re reading what’s left after I
gave up trying to be known.

These are not just words.
These are all the me
that bled quiet
while all else got to talk.

You left like it was nothing.

And now I feel everything.

I begged, you sighed.

I cried, you scrolled.

I stayed,

you left.

VIV

You Still Think I Was the One Who Ruined It?

You say I wrecked it all. You Truely think so. I don't get how, after all I did, you see me as the bad guy. Do you know what it's like? In a bond where I say sorry for each fight, not due to my fault. But, 'cause I feared to lose you, the one I called home. You did not see, but I was fading slow. I was in tears with texts, voice notes, and with no words. Each time, I hoped you'd get it. But you saw me as trouble. As drama. As if I broke your calm. I did not. I just begged for love in back. You say I wrecked us. I made a one-month tie last nine. Nine months of begging. Nine months of cling when you left many times. Each time you said, "I'm done," I ran back. And you think I caused the end? What did I wreck? I did not cheat. Not break your trust. I did not yell. I did not hit. I did not fight back when a mate hit me lots in rage. I was still sorry - for their rage. 'Cause that's me. Someone who craved peace. With you? I wanted love, not war. You said I'm too soft. That I made a big deal. That I was fake soft. But soft was all I had left. You gave me no hint I was your love. I felt like an extra in your life. One who cried too much to earn respect. And when I broke down - after six months to talk, hoping you saw what we had…

You were cold: “I have a boyfriend now.” And it was him. The one I warned you of. The one we fought over. One you backed as I felt fear. Fear of this very thing. Yet… I hid the pain. Still, I said I love you. Still, I tried. But you? You brought up your past as if I was not there. You spoke of how your ex kissed you, I know you didn’t wanna do that but I was your boyfriend it’s natural to get jealous. And I asked, “Why tell me this?”

You did not care. When I cried, no hug from you. You put me down. Compared me to him. Said I was worse than one who cheated on you, thrice. Worse than one who forced you. Worse - 'cause I was just true. And when I felt fear? When I spooked at losing you once more? You left me - once more. Said it was all my fault. Said I wrecked it all - once more. You said: “I’ll show you how I treat my last pick.” And you did. Made me feel like trash. Like a blunder. Like love was not for me. You were kind to others. You gave them your time, your softness, your sorry. But with me, I had to plead. Just to be heard. Just to be seen. I kept saying sorry. Even when I was the one in tears. Even when I was the one hurt. Even when your new love knew all ‘bout me - our chats, my voice notes, my pain. How did that happen? I still did not hate you. Even now. Even after threats.

Even after harsh words. Even when you did not care as I begged you to come back. Do you know how it felt, seeing you say "I love you" to him? After all the nights I wept for you? After all my "please come back's? After each time I saw you leave no guilt on your face? And you still say I wrecked it. You still think that? You'll say I penned this to seem good. To seem the hurt one. But the truth is - I was not faking. I was just trying. Way more than one should. And I guess... maybe I did wreck something. Maybe I broke myself trying to love someone who was not there to love me back.

This is not to blame you. This is not for show. This isn't to look clean or pure. This is my truth. It's for the girl who knew me well. You may not trust these words. But I did not write for trust. I wrote it so my misunderstood heart could be seen one last time. If you look for my flaws, you'll see them. If you seek your guilt, you might feel it. But if you read with the heart that loved me – maybe, you'll grasp the boy in the mess.

You said I seem pure. That I hide in soft words and smiles. Maybe I failed to show you more. Maybe my way of love was too quiet for you. Each time you doubted me, I broke inside. Not cause you hurt me. But 'cause I was trying so hard to love you my way— and it made you doubt me all the time. You thought I tricked you. That I acted like a victim. That I made faults and then wore pain as a mask. But the truth is, I was just broken in places I couldn't explain. When I worried, when I feared, when I snapped—it wasn't 'cause I didn't care. It was 'cause I cared too much and didn't know how to face losing you. I wasn't faking good. I was just trying to keep you. You said I hurt you. Maybe I did—by my silence, by my acts, by the pain I couldn't sort. But you didn't see my pain. How I stayed up late, torn, after our fights.

How I blamed myself all the time. How I stood up for you when friends asked why I stayed. I may not have been perfect, but I was true. And yes—I hated that guy. The one who flirted with you. I was mean for your sake, not for control. I saw what you didn't. I saw how his charm became comfort. And now he's with you.

He's the one I tried to block. I wasn't weak—I knew. And yet, I was cast as the bad one, for shielding what I thought was ours. I didn't cheat. I didn't lie. But you felt unloved. and I still can't see how. I thought I gave you all. Maybe too much of what wasn't right. Maybe I didn't see what you needed. But I always gave. When you said you had a new man— my heart didn't just break. It froze. Not 'cause you moved on. But 'cause I saw you never really knew me. You saw an image of me. Onc that was never real. And the boy who loved you—fully, foolishly, for you—was lost in your doubt. This book isn't revenge. It's not my tale. It's my goodbye. To all the words I kept inside. To all the love you didn't see. To all the ways you got me wrong, got me mixed up, judged me. I hope one day you see I wasn't faking. I was coming apart. And I hope— just for a moment— you miss the boy who'd do anything just to be enough for you.

You can't know what it did when you went mute. Not mad or done—just cold. You did not leave me crying. You left me in still air. and silence cuts deep. I was not just after your eye. I begged to not fade like I was just a trend, a slip, a name you wish you forgot. You did not just go. You fell apart—bit by bit—till I was left with a ghost who called me "baby." I kept thinking, "She's mixed up, she'll see it." But what kind of love lets you vanish so quick... and feel no pain?

I did not want you flawless. I just needed to feel cherished. Like I was not just extra weight. I showed you all my soft bits, those no one saw. I held on when you got dark, when you kept quiet, when you said, "don't want to talk." I stayed when you snapped. I was there through doubts, the gaps, the tough times you hid. and still—when I needed you most, you were not just gone... you were cold. You acted like I was the issue for caring a lot, for feeling too loud, for hurting when hurt.

Do you grasp what it's like to weep over someone who's good without you? One who was your all—the late texts, your haven—and now they don't ask if you ate. I wept so much some nights I shook.

My heart ached as though pressed down on. Yet, I told no soul. I hid their faults. Even as you left me behind, I kept you safe. Even as you made me feel dispensable, I prayed no one would snub you like that. That's how deeply I loved you. That's how I lost myself.

You always said, "I'm just off right now." and I got it. Each time. But when I was not okay, you blamed me for being too much. When I broke and said, "I fear I'm losing you," you saw me as a snag, not a heart to cuddle. I begged without words but with my quiet, my long texts, my deep thoughts, my sorrow—but you did not see. You did not see me. Truly. You saw what you chose. and when I became too true, too soft, too real… you left.

You did not just walk out. You made me rethink what love meant. You made me think being kind was not good enough. Maybe tears are weak. Maybe begging is low. You made me loathe how I loved. Now? Now I flinch when called sweet. Now I doubt all kind words. Now I rethink each reply. You moved on. You laughed anew. You slept at ease. and I stayed—mourning something you buried and didn't even pay your last respects.

I gave a part of me that won't go to another ever again. I can't love like I did with you again. That naive, hope-filled love that didn't need words, just your name. I wrote poems for you as if to stay alive via verse. Now each poem I write feels like pain. You broke me in ways none saw. No marks. Just an empty soul acting fine so no one asks, "Still sad over her?"

I'll never get how one can see you fall apart and not blink. How one can hear you cry and still say, "need space." You didn't kill me, but you made me wish I was someone else—someone who did not feel so much. Someone who did not care. Someone who could erase you like you did me.

I kept trying to show I was worth it. That I mattered. and perhaps that was my big error—thinking love had to be proved when it should have been safe.

You don't know this, but some nights I'd just lie on the ground. No tunes. No light. Just my thoughts choking me. Thinking of what I did wrong. Why I was not enough. Why you could love someone else so quick after saying I was your world. I was not perfect, but I never left you. Not once. But you… you left the moment it was not easy.

You'll move on. Maybe you have. You'll find one who doesn't weep before you, who doesn't overthink, who doesn't love with shaky hands and 3 a.m. poems. But you'll never find one who loved like I did—selflessly, foolishly, fully. and maybe one still night, you'll think of me. Not 'cause you miss me. But you'll know I was the only one who begged to stay, even while crumbling.

I don't think I can all say how it felt—seeing one I loved so much... just pull away. No noise. No care. As if it was all okay. You used to say I was a big deal. That I was rare. That I was not like the rest. But when it was time to show it, you made me feel like a weight you had to drop. I don’t even hate you for going. I just hate how easy you left. How fast you ran to someone else—someone I did not see as a risk because I had too much trust in you. . . . . .

I lost more than you. I lost me too. I stared in the glass and could not see the man I was. I was proud once of my way of love. Soft. Slow. Rich. But the way you took that love… it left me sad to have it. You did not hurt me with rage. You left me with cool. That kind of quiet—where you stop all, stop share, stop care—is way more loud than a fight ever was. . . . . .

I made wrong moves. I thought too much. I felt too much. I struck out at times when I should’ve heard more. But all I did wrong was from loving you so much it scared me. I was scared I'd lose you. I was scared to be wrong read by the one I let in so close. And maybe I was too full of feels, too soft, too safe—but not for a beat, was I not true.

I never left you. Not in those times you made me feel not wanted. I still tried. And now I wish I had not. For you did not try back. You just left. . . . . .

and the worst part? You didn't just move on. You went to him. The one guy I tried to save you from. The same guy I did not trust. The one who hit on you when we were still a thing. The one I stood up to—not from no trust, but from fear.
Fear that he was set for me to fail. Fear that you'd forget how I loved you and fall for the kind of love he sold: short, loud, and fake . . . . .

I think of when I spoke for you, not as a bossy guy, but as one who can't stand the thought of you with one who thought you were just a notch. You used to fight me on how I dealt with it. But I did it for I cared—I saw what you didn't. and now, the mad twist? He's the one who gets to keep the heart I kept like my own. . . . . .

It was not about him. It was not ever about him. It was about you not seeing why I did what I did. It was about me not being heard, even when I cried out in quiet.

I would've rather burnt on my own than watch you by some other's light. . . . . .

You never got how hard it was for me to trust. And when I did, when I gave you all of me, you used my flaws as your way out. You saw my worry as a bug. My sad as drama. My faith as a cage. And my love as "too much." But all I yearned was to be enough. . . . . .

Do you know what it's like to love one so much, you forget how to ask for love back? To give into one who stopped seeing you? I used to stay up to make sure you slept good. I used to read and re-read your notes as if they were truth. I used to give up myself to keep your world whole. And in the end, the hands that held you were left cold, lost, and unseen. . . . . .

You didn't just break my heart. You broke the man in me that held on. . . . . .

Now I'm with folks and still feel like I'm by myself, just for your name to pop up on my phone. I fake laughs at jokes I don't hear.

I breathe in a shell that still shakes each time someone hugs me—‘cause I found out how the kindest touch can fade the min you need it. . . . . .

And yet after this… I still care. That’s what hurts so much. Even after what you did, I don't seek payback. I just wanted to be enough. I just wanted to be the one you stuck with. The one you did not drop for one you once said you’d leave out. . . . . .

I don’t know if you’ll ever get what you did. But I hope—on some lonely night, when all else is fine—you feel it. That sharp, not known hurt. That gap you can’t name. And I hope you at last know the cost to be left by someone who never wished to leave.

I still call you
in my sleep.
Not to get you back,
just to hear
how love used to sound
before it left.

They said I'd find love once more.

But I was not on the hunt

for "love."

I sought **you**

in an else's quiet.

You were not there.

You did not break my heart.
You took it.
And when you laughed with him,
you crushed it
a bit more
under your foot.

I wiped your pics.

But not the act

of keying your name

at 2:17 a.m.,

just to see if you were

still

here

without me.

I'd have died
if you asked soft.
That's how much
I loved you.
That's how slight
you got it.

The hurt
is not in the bye.
It's in the months prior
when I said
“What’s wrong?”
and you said
“None.”
But all was gone by then.

I sought not the fault-free.
I just longed to be
your rest.
But I turned the cause
you sighed
and not smiled.

I saw you today.

Not face to face.

In a laugh

that did not come back to me.

You were not mine.
I just had your love
'til one
cooler, smarter,
more chic
came by knock.

Tell him—

the new guy—

that I held you

when you wished to vanish.

I was the fool

who loved your flaws

like stars.

Will he do so too?

I miss you.

Not like a love.

Like a cut-off arm

misses its hand.

Like a name

misses its call.

You sought one
less full of feel,
less strong,
less broke.
I sought one
who didn't pull back
when I wept.

You looked so cool
when you said
“We don’t work.”
I did not cry.
Not with you.
Just in my room,
each night then.

You kissed me once
as if I might break.
Then dropped me
as if it did not count
if I broke.

Your lack
has a smell.
It's burned notes,
slow replies,
and me
choking
in a space full of
your past.

I gave you
the soft me.
Now I keep back
even my nice
cause it brings back
the guy
you left.

You don't know
what it's like
to talk to a wall
wishing it turns
into your arms once more.

You smiled at me
like I was a tale
you once loved.
Now
the pages are marked
with quiet.

I'll never love like I did her. It's not a poem. It's a truth that hurts non-stop.

I go to bed, knowing the girl who once made me her world now hates me more than the quiet where I weep. Each night ends with thoughts that won't calm.

I stare in the mirror and I can't see me – the guy who changed, bent, softened all his sharp bits just to be safe to love.

Some other man will live the life I once dreamt of with her. He'll call her baby. He'll hear the laugh I tried so hard to keep safe. He'll get the her I lived for.

And I'll just… exist.

No one cares about how you feel until your sad turns to mad. Then, you're the bad guy in the tale you wrote to make it through.

I still miss those night calls. The silly jokes. The way her voice said my name, like it meant something.

She says it was pride. But if she came back, I'd kiss her feet for all to see just to touch her hand once more.

She thinks I forgot her – but it's 3 a.m., and I'm still looking at her pics, but she doesn't look back.

I gave her a love I never got, and she gave me a hurt I never sought.

I'm doing my best. But life keeps giving me hits like I earned them.

"Sleep, bro," they say. But, how can I sleep when the girl who was my calm now smiles at some other guy's texts?

I still think of how sweet she was at the start – like she knew how to love till she forgot how to stay.

Maybe the worst part? She left me so slowly that now no other girl feels like home.

And I know… I'll never love anyone again as I did her. But God, how I wish she saw how much that meant.

I was not perfect.
But I stayed.
Even when to stay
meant to break a bit
each day.

If sob made noise,

you would've stopped me sooner.

I still write verse
you'll not see.
Cause to love you
did not need
a crowd.

My mates say

you weren't worth it.

But if than you

was a slip,

then I wish

I stay dumb.

I loved you

like rain likes droughts—

eager,

worthless,

wishing

to count for a thing

to one

long dry.

Each bye

you said

came after a

"just playin."

Til the day

it did not.

When you left,

I didn't plead.

My eyes did.

Do you miss me

when it's too late to text?

Or is that a treat

you just spared

for the next?

I heard your laugh today—
not for real,
in mind.
And it still
tore a hole
in my heart.

You made me think
that to beg
was a way to love.
So I begged.
Til I lost
what pride was.

I burned my tongue
on each word
I held in for you.
And now,
even quiet
tastes like
your bye.

I hope he's good to you.

Not ’cause I want you to be happy.

But 'cuz’

I hope to think

my hurt

was worth it.

You didn't break up with me.
You just stopped
saying I was yours
till I had to call myself
alone.

You never slammed the door.
You just left
and let it stay open
so I'd keep thinking
if you'd come back.

I was that boy
who held your rage
as if it was holy.
Now I just hold
the quiet
as if it's a penalty.

I gave you poems.

You gave me

"seen."

Fair swap, right?

You didn't forget me.
You just loved
someone else
so loud
to mute
what we had.

The last look you gave me,

it was not love.

It was

"what do you want now?"

Do you remember
how I'd say
"don’t leave me on read"?
Now you just leave me
on memory.

My big mistake
was to think
you were soft
just cause you kissed me
like a lullaby.

He must be better, right?

He doesn’t cry.

He doesn’t beg.

He doesn’t write poems

at 3 a.m.

He just wins.

You looked so fair
when you hurt me.
Maybe that's why
I let you
again and again.

I don’t hate you.
I hate that I still
open your chat
to look at
“Last seen.”

If I could go back,
I'd pick you again.
Even if I knew
you'd leave again.

You promised always.
Then left when I cried
too much.

When I told you
"I feel less,"
you said nothing.
That quiet
told me all.

He held your hand
out loud.
I held your ache
in quiet.

I saw your story today.

Smiling, bright,

real.

I thought

if you missed

the boy

who showed you

how to smile

that way.

You said I thought too much.
But my thoughts
kept me from breaking
out loud.

Some nights,

I wish to forget your voice.

But my heart

still talks in it.

You called me too much.
Then loved a boy
who shows his love
in words.

I asked once.

Then twice.

Then each day.

Until my pride

was the price

you never asked for.

You said you missed me
but said no more.
That's when I knew—
missing
was just a word for you
when dull.

Do you sit in quiet
and hear my name
ring
like it used to?

I broke so soft,
you didn't see
you stood
on the scraps.

I wasn’t the top.
But I was the boy
who stayed
through your quiet,
still smiling
like he didn’t bleed.

The way you stopped loving me
was so hushed,
I didn't twitch.
I just vanished
like a whisper
you once loved.

You kept saying,
"I'm just not okay now."
But I was in the "now,"
and I never asked who hurt
you 'Cause I knew
it was me.

When I held you,
I didn’t think
you were short-term.
But maybe
you were just
a goodbye
set to happen.

I wasn't jealous
of his looks.
I was mad
you never smiled
at my name
like you do
at his texts.

I recall how
your fingers typed
"take care"
after our last fight.
As if
letting go of me
was just
another kind act.

Some nights,
I kiss your name
in my mind.
Not out of hope.
Out of habit.

You called it "space."

I called it

slow end with no reason.

The bad part is not
that you left off loving me.
It's that
you did not say when.

When you left,

you took no things.

Save for

the me that could still grin.

You said
"I do not want to talk now."
I thought it meant
"maybe soon."
But you
meant for good.

I did not chase you
out of low self-worth.
I chased you
because to lose you
felt like the end.

I miss you in waves.

But now,

the tide won't pull back.

He may make you laugh.

I made tears fall.

So you went.

Though

I was the one

who wept more.

You asked for room
but did not come back
to fill it.

In your new life,
I hope there's a spot
full of things
you kept—
things that hold
my scent.

I loved you
like a vow.
You loved me
like a might.

You moved on.

That's okay.

But how did you grin

so soon

while I was yet

trying to breathe

just fine

by myself?

I was not your wrong.

I was your **teach**.

But I wish

you were kind

as you taught it.

You knew
I had no else.
But yet
you left me
as if I'd cope.

I kept asking,

"Is something up?"

You said,

"No, all's good."

But now I see—

you were just planning to go in peace.

You once called me
"yours."
Now I'm
just a lad
who texts too much
and means too slight.

I miss being loved
by the you
who still held
to forever.

You made my name

a sore

I can't say

without a break.

I heard you got someone
who brings you peace.
I was just
a storm
in my own heart.

You said I was too much.
But you missed
how much of "me"
was just trying
to keep
"us."

Each day,
I wake
and forget
for two ticks
you're not mine.
Those two ticks
are all I have now.

I wiped your number.
But my fingers
still know it
like a scar.

You did not end me.
You just gave me
a life
I don't wish for now.

You were the air,

not just a craving.

I can live with no

vice.

But not

even air.

I check your page

less now.

Not as I'm done.

But as

it aches too much

when I do.

I was not asking for forever.

Just some more time.

Just one more

"night, dear."

Just one more

day

of being

not left out.

I recall
how soft you spoke
when mad
but still clung to me.
Now your soft
is for another.

You said
I was all gloom.
But dear,
you were the rain
on my lone spark.

You took him
not as he's top.
You chose him
as I made love hard.

My frame still acts
to your name
like a quiet shot
sent right
into my heart.

I hope

he won't need

to plead you to stay.

And if he does—

I hope

you can see

what you did to me.

You had all of me — not the right pieces, not the neat ones You had the messy, lost, scared, broke boy who still picked you with all his heart. and maybe that's why you could not see the love. It was not quiet and sweet. It shook, feared, too much, scared to lose you. and I did. I lost you. But not all at once. I lost you in the deep breaths, in the slow replies, in the soft no care you said wasn't there. and by the time you said you found someone new, my heart had died lots of times by your side. I did not try to seem not at fault. I just was not fake. You saw soft and thought it was a lie. You thought I used sad to avoid blame. But I did not know how to lie to you—I could not ask for what I liked. When I lost it, it was from fear. When I drew back, it was from doubt. and still, I stayed. Through the hard times. Through the doubts. Through the tired of not being got even when I yelled with no sound. You thought I was just putting on a show. I was just slowly breaking, right in front of you. and the worst part? You liked those who just liked your eyes, and doubted the one who would pick you in each real world. You thought I was bossy, too much, shy. I was just scared. Scared to lose you to someone I saw near, someone you said you would never like that way. and then, you gave him what you kept from me: calm, wait, your soft.

You gave him the good faith, while I had to say why for each tear as if it was a crime. You said I was the hurt one. But I was not just showing. I was living through a love that slipped no matter how soft I held it. I know I messed up. I got too sad. I fought back when I should've stopped. But my heart was still with you. Not even when yours was gone. I did not try to win fights.

I tried to stop us from growing apart. I did not act to have power—I acted 'cause I felt weak watching one I loved grow cold. You did not just go. You went on with one I once feared. One I saved you from. One who hit on you while I kept mum out of care. One I pushed back for us—but you went to him the moment I broke. No, this is not payback. It's the last rest. A place where I left each word I could not say, each me you could not love, each "don't go" you did not hear. This is not a love tale. It's a look into. Us. Me. All that should have been fixed but got left instead. You'll say you did not mean to hurt me. But you did. You'll say you thought I was faking it. But I wasn't. and maybe one day, when it's still... you'll think of the boy who cried to be got. and at last see him. Not as the bad one. Not as the false one. But as a man who just wanted to be loved like he loved you…

This wasn't for closure. This was for truth...

I hope you don't feel
what I felt
when you said
"go away"
in that same voice
you'd once say
"I love you."

You didn't just leave.

You

wiped me out

from your laughs,

your plans,

and your next day.

I sent,

"I miss you."

You sent back,

"Don't be a show-off."

and that stung

more

than no word.

I lost

12 years of mates

for you.

You dropped

me

like I was a joke.

You once said,

"I’m so glad to have you."

Now you act

like I’m the cause

you can't breathe.

It wasn't the split
that wrecked me.
It was
how quick
you swapped
what we had.

You didn't move on.

You **bolted.**

and I stayed back

folding your thoughts

into 'I'm sorry' notes

I won’t send.

Do you recall
how tight I held you
when your world
broke down?
Do you recall
how fast
you let mine go?

I saw my face today.

And I could not name

the boy

you forgot.

He shares clips

with your hand in his.

and I wonder

if he knows

those hands

once dried

my tears.

You made me seem
like a bad guy
for asking
"why did love end?"

I never wished for all time.

Just truth.

Just real talk

before you left.

You broke me
in slow steps.
So I couldn't yell.
Just
silently fade.

I still whisper
“goodnight”
to the dark.
As if
you might answer
from where
you forgot me.

You said

"I’m not set for love."

Yet your grin

yelled

someone else is.

I was a poet.

You were my spark.

But you loathed

every word

that hinted at

you going.

You hated it

when I wept.

So I learned

to shatter

eyes wide

and mouth shut.

I wish one day
someone holds me
with the calm
I aimed to give you
as I was sinking.

I shared all.
Even the bits
I hid from.
and you used
each one
to back
leaving.

You cut me off
everywhere.
But I still spot you
in sunsets,
coffee mugs,
mirrors.
You left me.
But not all let go.

They say I'm lucky
I ran.
But love
doesn't feel free
when you were
the safe place.

He may know
your top songs now.
But he’ll never hear
how they felt
when you hummed them
on my chest.

I guess

you share with him

your secrets

like

you used to with me—

hoping the breeze

won't bring them back.

I wish

you came with a note:

"Will go

when you fall

too deep."

Even my shrink

can't tell

how I still

guard you

from my own hurt.

I hope your new flame

doesn't write.

Because

if he does,

you'll ignore

my poems

like I was just

a warm-up.

I’m not mad you left.
I’m mad
you made it seem
like I earned it.

Some nights
I fake a smile
so my folks don't fret.
They don't know
your name
sticks
in my throat
like a rock.

I begged you

to chat.

Now

I beg me

not to recall.

You didn’t just
split up.
You buried me
with a grin
and walked off
as if
nothing
was gone.

I didn't need
your whole world.
Just the spot
where I didn't have to beg
to be loved.

I used to be your top pick.

Then I turned

"someone who speaks too much

about his thoughts."

I saw you
fall out of love with me
as if it was a task
you couldn't skip
any more.

They said,

"Time cures all."

But it's been months

and I still taste

you

in my tears.

I loved you loud.
You left
in silence.

My last word to you
was six parts long.
Yours?
"Okay."

I can't unlearn
how your voice
used to say
"baby."
It's sewn
in my back.

You made me feel
tough to love.
But I was only hard
to trick.

You’re not a past thought.

You’re a cut

that keeps bleeding

even after

I forget

how it started.

I wish he loves

your bad bits

with the same hands

I used

to calm your storms.

The worst part?
You never even asked
why I was crying.

I gave you
everything.
And you gave him
your next days.

You used to cry
when I was sad.
Now you cry
when I talk.

I don't need you back.

I just want

who I was

before I lost you.

You were not
just my girl.
You were
my twin.
And now I don't know
who I am.

The day you left,

I told myself,

"She'll know."

You never did.

I saw
our past times
turn into proof
you used
to back
leaving me.

I quit writing poems
for weeks.
As each line
was asking you
to come back.

You didn't lose like.

You just found someone

easier

to love.

You left in quiet.
But your hush
still yells
like a shout
in every bit of me.

I don't trust in ghosts.
But I still rest
on the left side
of the bed.

I loved you

with no pride.

You loved me

with no break.

Until

you did.

Your last words to me
were,
"Let's just end this."
As if
this
wasn't the only thing
that kept me here.

You gave me
a life of hurt
in a three-month tie.

You said
I was too much.
But my chest
still tightens
when I hear
your name.

He’s your calm now.

I was just

the fight

you never wished to have.

I cut your photos.

But I can’t cut

the act

of loving you.

I used to wish
you'd come back.
Now I hope
you don't come back
too late.

I loved you
like faith.
You loved me
like a fad.

Some part of me
is still here
for the you
who held me
like I was the only thing
that made sense.

You left me
with no clear answers
and a form
that still shrinks
at your name.

They say,

"If she wished to,

she would."

and that's how I knew

you didn't.

I begged for you
with pure truth
than ever in prayer.

You thought I was weak
'cause I cried.
But tears
were the only thing
holding me
together.

I never shared
what it was like
when you stopped calling me
"mine."
It still
feels like
a loss.

You didn't break my heart.

You just

left it to rot

in your quiet.

Even now,

when one asks

if I've moved on—

I just smile.

How do I tell

you're still

inside my lungs?

You were the sun.
I was glass
trying to hold you.
Now all I have
is warmth
and glass.

I cried beside you.

Not to trick—

just to show

I was real.

He must think

you’ve always been sure.

So calm.

He won't know

you got that

on the brink of my tears.

I gave you
a love note
with my blood
not ink.
You closed it,
smiled,
and left.

You used to say,
"I love your way of love."
Then one day,
you didn't.
Like my love
was too much
for you.

I blocked you once.

Not from hate.

Just so I wouldn't

look you up

ten times each day

and feel worse.

You showed me
how quick one can
be swapped.
Now I question
mirrors.

You laughed at my poems
the last time I showed you.
Not 'cause it was fun.
'Cause you
were not
the girl in them anymore.

I sought a good end.
You left me
a still chat
and a happy tale
with another.

I still say
"goodnight"
to no one.
That’s
how I recall
you were.

You made me fall for
fixing you.
But when I needed aid,
you went
'cause I wasn't "fun now."

I think

if he knows

you once said

"I'll never go."

Right before you left.

You told me
you were tired.
I didn't know
you meant
tired of me.

He has your future.

I hold your vows.

Guess who's in more pain?

You didn’t just
end it with me.
You broke
the boy
who thought
he could mend things.

I still guard you

in rooms

where no voice is heard.

As my head

is the noisiest court

and you

are always

judged.

You told me to move on
as if easy.
Yet I’m still searching
for the way
to forget your name.

You found someone new.
I broke down
with someone old—
me.

If loving you

was a cut,

I kept it open

for the hurt

was all

you left me.

You were my lesson.

I was

your hurt.

You don't miss me.

You miss

how fast

I forgave you.

At times,

I think

if your new love

knows

he stands

where I once

knelt.

You didn’t wreck me.

You turned me

into a show

of what love

shouldn't feel like.

You were not my first love.

But you were my last hope.

They asked my type.
I said, "One who won't leave
when I break."

You cried when you were sad.

I heard.

I cried when I broke.

You left.

I wish I could hate you.
That would be less hard.
Than to write poems
to one who won't
read them.

I told you

I feared losing you.

You did not help me.

You just

began to go.

He might not know

how many nights

I lost sleep

just to hear you breathe.

I wrote for months

metaphors for you.

Yet no line

hurts more

than your quiet.

You were not cold.

You were

gone

and still just said

"hmm."

I loved you
on days
you made me
hate me.

You knew
how much I cared.
That made it
easy
for you
to look past me.

When you said,

"I need time,"

I stopped my world.

You played

with someone else.

I still use
the right side of the bed.
But your side
has been
empty
for months.

You never had to ask
me to stay.
I was there.
But you stopped
seeing me.

You left

because I was too much.

But I was that way

because I knew you'd leave.

I kept your texts.
All of them.
They are the last bits
of love
that did not last.

I did not lose you.

I lost

the me

who thought

of good ends.

You didn't say bye.
Your words
got short
until you gave
no reply.

I begged you

to get it.

Now I beg me

to forget

my care.

You were my calm
and my fight.
But more
the quiet
after the fight.

I hope you don’t cry

like I did.

But if you do—

I hope

one helps.

You asked why
I thought too much.
Even forever felt
short with you.

No need to block me now.
I'm gone
in your world
already.

Each "good morning"

was yours.

Now mornings seem

like goodbyes

to dreams you left.

I aim to forget you.
But your name
still sounds like
home.

You told me

to move on.

But you missed—

I held not to you.

But to the joy

you brought.

I said
you keep me here.
You just sent
a thumbs up.

My songs were

about love.

Now they show

I survived you..

No need to say
why you went.
Your joy
spoke loud.

I'd like to say

I'm done missing you.

But that's

a lie

to keep me alive.

One day
you'll think of me.
And then,
I hope
you feel
a small hurt.

LASTLY…

I can't recall
what calm is like.
Just your voice
leaves an echo
in every bit of me
that still hopes
you'll return.

I gave up on closure.
You handed that
to another.

You stay quiet now.
But my heart still
writes your name —
like it unlocks
something warm.

I don’t pen poems now—
I just bleed softly
into lines
no one sees
but me.

You left me
like closing an app
— fast and quiet.
Cool.
Fast.
Gone.

I wish
you wept
when you left.
But you did not.

I did.

I wept
for us both.

I still view your page.
Not to see if you miss me.
Just to make sure
that you do not.

At times I think,
did I even mean
a thing
to you?

If I did—
how could you let go
so fast?

You broke me,
not like a blaze.
No.
You broke me slowly
— like rain does to rooftops
Gentle.
Steady.
Soft.

Till all fell down
in silence.

And the hard part is—
I still love you.

And I might always.

Even when I’m old,
creased,
laughing with another,
your name
will still feel like
a secret
I kept on
saying.

A NOTE JUST FOR YOU

If you see this,
you might think
I'm acting pure.
That I'm the sad one,
as usual.

But that's not it.

This isn't to blame you.
This isn't to save me.
It's about love—
the kind that had me cry
at 2 a.m.
and still
hope for your name on my screen.

I know we both had flaws.
I know I begged too much.
Wept too loud.
Held too close.

But all that
was not to own you.
It was since
you were my peace
in a world so wild.

You might still feel
I played games,
or was too much,
or just too feeling.
But I hope,
at least once,
you saw the lad
who would've died
just to hear
"I'm proud of you."

I didn't jot all this
to get you back.

I wrote it
as I still care.
Even after all,
I wish you

to recall me
as the lad
who loved you
so much
he forgot
how to breathe
without you.

If I was wrong,
I'm sorry.
If I hurt you,
I'm sorry.
But I did not fake it.

I meant each poem.
Each word.
Every time I said,
"I'd do all for you."

Take care.
Really.
You'll always hold
a soft spot
in the lad

you thought

was easy

to leave.

I never hated you.

Even when you forgot I was still hurting.

– V

If you ever read this,

I hope you cry too.

I don't know if you'll read this. And if you do, I don't know what you'll think. You'll say I play it sweet. Act like I'm soft. Make it all about my hurt. But I swear, this ain't about me. It's about all I held in while trying to love you right. All I kept in 'cause I was scared you'd leave me soon. I once thought love meant you try hard. So I gave my all. Even when it meant I had to chase. Even when I lost who I was. Even when I cried and you looked away. You know, when I texted you after 6 months... I hoped you'd see. I thought you'd know what we had. I hoped for warmth. A past. A flash. But I got a line that hit like a shot: “I have a boyfriend.” Not just any guy. But the one I once told you to watch. The one I'd snap at from your phone, not out of spite— But 'cause I was scared. 'Cause I was your man, and he was never just “nice.” But when I got mad, you left me. You fought me. You said: “Kar diya na usko mad.” As if his mood beat my place in your life. Then... You spoke of your ex. How he kissed you. How you rode bikes with him. How he held you and tried more. And I thought—why tell me this? Don't you see I hurt just hearing his name? When I said it hurt, you did not hug me. You did not say sorry. You yelled at me. Like I was a kid in the way. Like my hurt was too much. And yet, I stayed.

I loved. I clung on. Even when I was your last thought, and you showed it with words I can't forget: “Ab dikhati hun mai apni last priority ko kaise treat karti hu.” And you did. You made me feel not real. I was the one who cried to you, shared my woes, hoped for a hug. And I left more hurt. Turned around. Made small. Muted. You never said "it's okay." You just made me feel too much. You said your ex cheated 3 times. And yet, you gave him 3 tries. But what did I get? Where was my shot? Where was my care? I recall your friend told me, his sis (you) was crying. But I cried too. Where was the ward for me? You made it seem like love was a fight I had to win with words, with my why's, with my hands shaking as I told why I was hurt. I wasn't too much. I was just loving one who didn't get my love. I kept going. You kept getting it wrong. I kept crying. You kept leaving. And I still thought: maybe one day she'll know what she had. But you never did. And now? Now I'm just the guy who cared too much. Loved too much. Stayed too much. And was too much left out.

And If This Book Finds You… Then I guess I've done what can't be took back. Not 'cause I wrote of you. But 'cause I wrote what you never wished to hear. Folks might call this a poem book. But in these pages, I think I just laid to rest a me that can't stay. So if you're reading this — and it feels heavy, feels wrong, feels like too much truth in too soft a voice… Maybe I didn't live out this tale like you thought. Maybe I didn't just write a book. Maybe I left a grave. And maybe what you hold isn't just sheets… Maybe it's proof that you'll never again talk to the me who still thought you loved him.

I wasn't acting.

I was breaking.

And maybe that's what hurt the most.

You never noticed the difference.

If she ever asks about me...

Tell her I finally stopped begging.

If you're still reading this…

I guess I committed emotional murder.

Sorry.

I didn't mean to break anyone.

I was just tired of breaking alone.

Goodbye…

ABOUT THE AUTHOR

VIV pens like silent would, if it could talk.

He won't say he's a poet – just a guy who felt a lot and had to share it.

His words won't mend you. They just keep you company when no one else will.

"She Left Like Sunday" is his first book.

He's probably overthinking on Instagram: ***@penmanviv***